Did You See That Rabbit?

by Anne Schreiber • Illustrated by Marcy Dunn Ramsey

SCHOLASTIC INC.

New York   Toronto   London   Auckland   Sydney
Mexico City   New Delhi   Hong Kong

Rabbits are fast.

They can hop, hop, hop.

Did you see that rabbit?
Where did he go?

Rabbits like plants.

They rip the tops.

Their teeth nip and chop.

Rabbits dig holes.

This rabbit hid his hole.
He drops plants on top.

What is down in the hole?
Rabbit kits!

A rabbit can have lots of kits.

This kit sips milk.
That kit hops and flops.

The rabbit and kits nap.

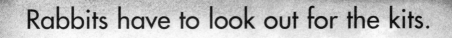

Rabbits have to look out for the kits.

Do you see the rabbit up on the hill?
She stops and sits still.
She sniffs.

The rabbit and kits come down—fast!

You can see rabbits out there.

You can see rabbits in here.

This rabbit will plop down on your lap.
You can pet him.

Did you see that rabbit?
He likes you!

RABBIT CHOW

CEDAR CHIPS

WATER

Phonics Booster 9

★ Words to Sound Out ★

/r/r	-op
rabbit	chop
ran	drops
rip	flops
	hop
	top

★ Words to Remember ★

come   down   out   up   where

★ Story Words ★

dig   here   hole   teeth   your